THE MOON OF THE
MONARCH
BUTTERFLIES

THE MOON OF THE
MONARCH
BUTTERFLIES

THE THIRTEEN MOONS

The Moon of the Owls (JANUARY)

The Moon of the Bears (FEBRUARY)

The Moon of the Salamanders (MARCH)

The Moon of the Chickarees (APRIL)

The Moon of the Monarch Butterflies (MAY)

The Moon of the Fox Pups (JUNE)

The Moon of the Wild Pigs (JULY)

The Moon of the Mountain Lions (AUGUST)

The Moon of the Deer (SEPTEMBER)

The Moon of the Alligators (OCTOBER)

The Moon of the Gray Wolves (NOVEMBER)

The Moon of the Winter Bird (DECEMBER)

The Moon of the Moles (DECEMBER-JANUARY)

NEW EDITION   THE THIRTEEN MOONS

THE MOON OF THE MONARCH BUTTERFLIES

BY JEAN CRAIGHEAD GEORGE

ILLUSTRATED BY KAM MAK

HarperCollins*Publishers*

The Moon of the Monarch Butterflies
Text copyright © 1968, 1993 by Jean Craighead George
Illustrations copyright © 1993 by Kam Mak

Typography by Al Cetta
1 2 3 4 5 6 7 8 9 10
NEW EDITION

Library of Congress Cataloging-in-Publication Data
George, Jean Craighead, date
        The moon of the monarch butterflies / by Jean Craighead
George ; illustrated by Kam Mak.—New ed.
        p.   cm. — (The Thirteen moons)
        Includes bibliographical references (p.   ) and index.
        Summary: Describes the female Monarch butterfly's solitary
flight from Arkansas to Michigan as she lays the eggs that will
hatch and repeat her life cycle.
        ISBN 0-06-020816-3. — ISBN 0-06-020817-1 (lib. bdg.)
        1. Monarch butterfly—Juvenile literature. [1. Monarch
butterfly. 2. Butterflies.] I. Mak, Kam, ill. II. Title.
III. Series: George, Jean Craighead, date, Thirteen moons
(HarperCollins)
QL795.B85G46   1993   91-33152
595.78′9—dc20   CIP
                                                              AC

Why is this series called The Thirteen Moons?

Each year there are either thirteen full moons or thirteen new moons. This series of books is named in their honor.

Our culture, which bases its calendar year on sun-time, has no names for the thirteen moons. I have named the thirteen lunar months after thirteen North American animals. Primarily night prowlers, these animals, at a particular time of the year in a particular place, do wondrous things. The places are known to you, but the animal moon names are not because I made them up. So that you can place them on our sun calendar, I have identified them with the names of our months. When I ran out of these, I gave the thirteenth moon, the Moon of the Moles, the expandable name December-January.

Fortunately, the animals do not need calendars, for names or no names, sun-time or moon-time, they follow their own inner clocks.

—JEAN CRAIGHEAD GEORGE

THE MOON OF MAY slipped below the curve of the earth a few minutes before dawn. Darkness engulfed the long, wide Mississippi River Valley.

In a damp field in Arkansas, in the brief blackness before daybreak, a dewy breeze arose. Scented with wet loam, sassafras leaves, and sweet-scented shrub, it blew through the woods and over a rice field, and faded in the river thickets. Then the sun came up.

Where the breeze had traveled, swatches of wildflowers were blooming. Violets, May apples, and columbine bounced on cool green stems; dogbanes, wild geraniums, irises, and buttercups sprang toward the sun. Apple flowers blossomed. Their petals fell like paper snowstorms. Pine and pecan blooms released their pollen, and the winged seeds on the maples spun as they ripened. The warm moist earth of May and the lengthening hours of light were renewing life all across North America.

The longer days triggered the birds to migrate. As far up the Mississippi River as Iowa, a sky tide of wings rolled northward night and day. They were the migrants that arrive on their nesting grounds in May—the bluebirds, warblers, thrushes, flycatchers, wrens, and orioles. A few days behind them came the indigo buntings and cuckoos, meadowlarks and spotted sandpipers. All the birds were flying in uncountable billions toward trees, grasslands, seashores, or little wooden boxes on poles—their summer nesting places. This migration that had begun slowly in January and February was now at its height.

Ribbons of wings streamed over the Mississippi River Valley and the Atlantic and Pacific coast-lines, which are the sky roads, called flyways, of the birds.

Beneath the birds, flying strong on paper-thin wings, went another migrant—a monarch butterfly. She had left her winter home in Mexico, flown across Texas, and was now traveling northeast on a straight line through Arkansas. She flew across open fields, over blooming peach trees and greening vineyards. She was on her way home to the faraway place in which she had been born—a meadowland near Toronto in Ontario, Canada.

The monarch had been flying for many days. This morning she had soared and flapped forty miles, crossing into Missouri at noon. She winged on, passing the smokestacks of Poplar Bluff, its shopping centers, churches, and railroad station. Before sundown she came to rest on a wisteria vine that entwined the porch of a small white house in the country. Clinging to a lavender flower, she closed her wings above her back, as butterflies do. Her wing tops were burnt orange, their undersides yellow. Black veins spread through them like lead in a stained-glass window. Their edges seemed as if the night and day had been knitted into them; they sparkled white and black. Her antennae were club-tipped wands that could smell flowers, feel obstacles, and help to orient her in flight.

The monarch was not as brilliant as she had been in September, when she had changed from her pupal stage into a butterfly. She had then set out on her long migration south, from Canada to the Lava Mountains of Mexico. There in a warm, moist forest she had overwintered with millions of other monarch butterflies, then started home to Canada.

The long flight had taken its toll on her. One wing was slightly torn, and many of the scales that colored her body and wings had fallen away.

Although she looked more fragile than when she had started, her pale wings and body were still incredibly strong and could easily carry her home.

Just before evening the butterfly sipped nectar from the wisteria flowers on the porch, uncurling her proboscis as she reached deep into their sweet pots. Then she rested. She was alone, for the spring migration of monarch butterflies is not as social as their autumnal flight, when thousands fly by day and gather together at night.

This journey begins when the coolness nips the land. Those butterflies that emerge before the killing frost of autumn take wing and hurry like leaves before the wind. Down the east and west coasts they fly by the millions along the ancient, invisible sky trails of the monarchs. Many go eighty miles before floating down to a tree to rest away the night with others of their species. The trees they choose are usually pines, maples, or willows—trees where their tiny feet can cling to the slender needles or the small notches in the

leaves. As the butterflies gather, the trees become spectacles of beauty. Firelike wings seem to set them aflame. They flicker yellow and orange. Once a tree is visited by monarchs, it becomes a butterfly tree and they may visit it every year—nobody knows how this knowledge is passed on.

At dawn the wisteria vine where the butterfly rested became a noisy place. Several dozen house sparrows chirped and fluttered their wings as they awoke. Their untidy nests, crammed into the dense vines, were filled with cheeping babies whose feathers were just breaking out of their stubby sheaths. The butterfly could not see the birds, for the sun was not bright enough to bring vision to her eyes. Each of her eyes is really thousands of eyes that make up one compound eye.

When at last she could see the flowers and sky, she opened her wings and flew. Soaring over a tall magnolia tree, she looked down on fading pink blossoms that once stood like china cups on short stems. Now the petals were falling to earth.

She did not stop to drink magnolia nectar, but she did sense it on the air with her proboscis, antennae, and feet, for these parts of the butterfly are its taste buds.

Still flying northeast, she came to Cape Girardeau in Missouri.

Below her in the marshy edges of the big Mississippi River, the eggs of spring peepers were hatching: Tiny polliwogs twisted and flipped as they broke through their egg cases and the walls of gelatin that had protected them while they developed. Free but tired, they sank to the food-filled bottom of the shallows.

In deeper water a male sunfish was just beginning to form his nest. He was sweeping the silt from a sandy bar, using his tail and fins as a broom. The butterfly did not see him or the ripple on the water made by his female as she circled down to examine his glittering saucer-shaped nest. In a few days she would lay her eggs

there, then swim away, leaving her mate to guard them from enemies and keep them clean of silt until they hatched. The fine sediment can smother and kill fish eggs.

Flying hard now, staying about twenty feet above the ground, the butterfly flew around factories and granaries, glided over houses and puddled country roads. She glanced down at the designs in the fields, looking for a very special shape and color—a milkweed plant. She came lower, feeling the pressure of an egg within her, an egg that must be laid on a milkweed and no other plant. The caterpillar that would hatch from it could eat no other food.

A male awaited her in a milkweed patch. She mated with him and flew deep into the patch. A tiny yolk within her was now covered with a strong shell in which there was a minuscule hole.

The butterfly alighted on the oval leaf of a young milkweed growing beside a country road.

She folded her wings above her back. As an egg left her body, it passed her sperm receptacle and was fertilized by way of the hole in the egg's shell. About as big as half a pinhead, the egg adhered to the leaf's undersurface. It glittered, for it was multifaceted, like a diamond. The butterfly left it on the leaf and flew on.

In a few days the egg on the milkweed would hatch. A tiny caterpillar, lavishly banded with white and greenish yellow, would open its jaws, feed on the eggshell, and bite into the tender leaf.

Eating almost constantly, the caterpillar would grow rapidly. In a few days its coat would split down its back and the caterpillar would step out of it a little larger and a little brighter in color. Now it would have black bands as well as the white and yellow ones. This molt would happen four times. At the last molt, usually after fourteen days, the caterpillar would be approximately two inches long.

This larger and more colorful caterpillar

would walk under a leaf on which it had been feeding. There it would spin and attach a silken pad to the leaf stem and grasp it with its two false rear legs that exist only in the caterpillar stage to hold up its long body. Letting go with its true front legs, it would hang downward in a J shape. Violently twisting, the caterpillar would shed its fifth coat, and there would be no more caterpillar.

In its place would be a green-gold case, studded with golden jewellike spots. In this—the chrysalis—the monarch butterfly would begin a miraculous change. Legs, head, and body would be reorganized.

After two weeks, the insect inside the case would turn dark red and the chrysalis coat would split. A delicate black leg would reach out. A pert head with big eyes and a coiled proboscis would emerge. Finally, the graceful insect, now splashed with black and white, would crawl out on the chrysalis and lift wing buds that look much

like the buds of flowers. The monarch would pump fluid into the buds, and they would unfold into four beautiful wings. When they dried, the monarch would fly, drink nectar, mate, and, if it was a female, bejewel the milkweed plants with the summer eggs of the species. Unlike her migrating mother, she would live only a few months.

It is the butterflies of August and September that live long lives—up to six months. They are the migrants. They must live through the winter in a moist warm climate in order to perpetuate their species. When they start off for their southern homes, they are not sexually developed; nevertheless, the sex of each migrant can be distinguished. The males have one black spot on each of their hind wings.

The migrants take a bearing on the sun to find their way. They look at the angle of light, turn, and lift their antenna. Then they take off on a beam that leads to their winter homes. In the west they fly from Canada down the coastal mountains to Palm Grove, California. In the east they travel from Canada and the eastern United States on a perfectly straight line to the Lava Mountains near Mexico City. Practically no monarchs live on the dry plains and midlands of the United States and Canada.

Having deposited her egg, the monarch took off to the northeast. She darted through a park near the outskirts of Evansville, Indiana, on the Ohio River. A boy jumped to catch her. She climbed away from him and skimmed the tree-tops. A wind blew her to the docks where people worked and back out over the water where barges and fishing boats moved.

Before dusk the butterfly saw the white line of a ship's railing below her. She dropped down to rest, not knowing she was hitching a ride up the Ohio River.

She closed her wings over her back. Along the quiet edges of the river where the water was shallow and moved slowly, bullhead catfish had gathered in couples to spawn and renew life. Some were making nests in the bank, digging with their mouths. They were picking up silt and spewing it into the current to be carried away. Other catfish couples had already laid eggs. Some nests were beside old logs, others in the round caves of sunken automobile tires.

One pair of parents was guarding a cluster of little black hatchlings inside a tire. As tiny as they were—about the size of a fly's leg—they looked like miniatures of their parents. Their faces were adorned with whiskers. Their back fins were oval, their skin slippery and seemingly scaleless. The tiny fish had lines down their bodies. These were their balancing organs and ears. Called lateral lines, they told the fish whether they were right side up or not. The lines also picked up distant sounds—a crayfish moving stones, an eel swishing down to eat them.

An hour later, when twilight darkened the

water, the father catfish nosed his children out of the tire. He followed the wheeling cluster as they went out into the weeds to feed. A hungry bass came toward them. The catfish father opened his jaws and sucked his fry into his mouth. He held them there until the bass swam on by. He would tend them in this manner until they were almost a half inch long; then he would swim away and leave them to fend for themselves. Even he would not recognize his offspring after they were independent. If they passed too closely, he would swallow them.

The monarch rode on up the Ohio River. Overhead hot and cold air collided, clouds formed, and rain splattered on the river and the valley. The butterfly crept under the boat railing and spent the rainy night clinging to a splinter by the hooks on the tips of her feet.

At dawn the boat pulled into the dock at New Albany, Indiana. The storm was over. The hills were wet with rain shine. Bright azaleas, which

had already bloomed and faded in Arkansas, were still flowering in cooler Indiana. Tree leaves were smaller here, for the warmth moved slowly up the continent.

The butterfly crawled up on the railing and found her position had changed in the night. She took another reading on the sun and flew toward the awakening town. She was back on course. She fluttered around the downtown buildings, flew on to the outlying railroad yards, and kept going. When she saw green patches of farmland below her, she came earthward.

A bluebird flew toward her. She was hunting insects for her young, but when she saw the black and orange colors, the bird darted away. The monarch butterfly is poisonous to birds, and they have learned to avoid it. The bluebird swerved and caught a crane fly. Alighting on a fence post, she slipped into a hole. A lusty chattering and chirping greeted the parent. Red mouths opened, and the bluebird fed one lively nestling. The

babies almost filled the hollow in the post, for they were fully feathered and ready to fly. Bluebirds nest early. Their babies would be taking short flights when the wood thrushes and orioles were still building their nests in mid May.

Near a red barn a vegetable garden was striped with the green sprouts of cucumbers and squashes. The first thick leaves of the melon plants stood boldy in the sun. Hard green strawberries gleamed among fringed leaves. Beyond the garden the rye was beginning to flower. The corn had just been planted.

The butterfly again flew down to lay another egg. Dropping among the blades of the foxtail grass, she found a young milkweed plant, laid an egg, and flew off into the wind. She passed a woods where a loose cluster of paper wasps was hovering around an elm limb. A small cluster of egg cells marked the beginning of their home. A few of the wasps had gathered the fibers of plants and were chewing them into a tough material

for more egg cells. Others were converting wood fiber into the gray paper that would encircle the wasp eggs like a castle wall.

Deeper in the woods the flowers of the tulip trees were sitting on short stems like orange-green fruit cups. The walnut and butternut trees were fragrant with spicy yellow-green flowers, and the feathery blossoms of the willows were drifting on the wind like a cloud of goose down.

A southwesterly breeze carried the butterfly on to the northeast. She soared over wild cherry trees where robins and blue jays were harvesting the first of the ripening fruit. She flew over roads that were bordered with blue wild phlox.

The next day she was southwest of Dayton, Ohio, and still flying northeast. A small milkweed plant attracted her, and she fluttered down upon it to lay another egg. The morning was warm, almost eighty degrees, and she was thirsty. She flitted to a flower and drank its nectar. Refreshed, she sailed above a dirt road that led through a hardwood forest of hickories, oaks, maples, and ashes.

A long-tailed weasel darted among the trees looking from right to left with quick flashes of her golden head. She had a long graceful neck and bright black eyes. Her belly was white, the tip of her tail black. In her mouth hung a baby, curled like a bud, its head tucked into its feet. Its eyes had opened only that day. Although it had been born in early April, it was not until this thirty-seventh day of its life that it could see. By the end of the May moon it would be weaned and, in a few more weeks, hunting mice and frogs on its own.

The mother weasel saw no dangers and carried her little one under the ferns and trillium leaves without stirring them. She emerged on the stream bank. Flowing over the stones, she disappeared into a den she had fashioned only last night. Early that evening she had felt a need to move her family and had made this den by the stream. The food was more plentiful by the waterway. She

put the baby in a leaf-lined nest deep in the embankment and went back for the others. When all were moved, she slept beside them, waiting until darkness to hunt food. She would move them again and again before they were independent.

As the butterfly flew along the road, a baby cottontail, no bigger than a human fist, came bounding out from under a bush. The cottontail hopped to the the woodland meadow to nibble a flowering chickweed. As she munched, three bright faces watched. The red fox's pups, still fuzzy with baby fur, still wobbly and awkward, studied the little cottontail. From the safe darkness of their den at the edge of the woods, they watched everything that moved—bees, birds, wind-blown flowers—and the cottontail. Presently they crawled back into their earthen den, for they were still too young to venture into the woods.

The woodland also hid skunk babies. One family was curled in the hollow of a fallen tree.

Only three days old, the babies were covered with black fuzz. On their backs could clearly be seen the white stripe of the skunk.

In the chamber of another woodland den, four baby chipmunks sat on their haunches near their mother. She gave them a signal, and with a bound, they ran up the long tunnel that led from their bedroom to the sunlight at the surface. They climbed onto a log, tails up like flagpoles, and boxed each other with their front paws. Then they rushed into the woods to stuff fallen maple seeds into their cheeks. Born in March, they were were now six weeks old and being weaned. Their mother was nursing them less and less, so they went farther and farther from home to investigate the woods and hunt for seeds and berries. This morning one stayed away until noon, then ran home with a cheekful of cherry seeds.

The butterfly flew on. She climbed above the forest and flew northeast until late afternoon. When the light grew too dim for her to see, she came to rest in a pine tree near a blue-fruited dogwood blooming in an abandoned field. The needles rustled, and a catbird landed on a limb below her. He jumped to another branch, then straightened his feathers and wiped his bill on a twig. He, too, had been traveling all day. In a last dash to get home to his abandoned field, he had flown two hundred miles. He was not out of breath, nor did his heart pound from the exertion of his long trip. His body, like the bodies of all birds, made adjustments to the demands of migration. He was feeling fine. He flitted into the center of the pine and listened to his woodland neighbors.

The green frogs were piping their evening song, and the wood thrush, which had arrived only a few days before, called out his first song of the season. Like the spilling of water, the clear notes of this beautiful bird poured forth. Then, at sundown, the wood thrush stopped singing. From a tall tree a phoebe called in the dusk. Presently, he too was quiet. The robins chirped on, then suddenly stopped. Each kind of bird has a curfew of light that silences it for the night. First the wood thrush is quiet, then the phoebe and robin. Finally, when these are silent, the pensive sweet carol of the wood pewee begins in the afterglow. When the song is done, it is night.

Darkness had come many hours ago for the butterfly, and she could not see the glow of the firefly in the grass blades below her. A female had turned on the light in the last four segments of her abdomen. Nearby, a male walked across a leaf. He did not glow, for he had just emerged from his pupal stage. His wings were small, his body fragile. He was not mature enough to shine. It would be late June before he would sparkle two consecutive flashes, the mating call of his species. He walked to the end of the leaf and rested.

The night passed quietly for the butterfly. When the May moon was setting and the sun coming over the edge of the world, the wood pewee began his song of the predawn. Next came the voices of the robin, the cardinal, the phoebe, and the wood thrush as, one by one, the birds awoke to their morning light alarm. The catbird listened and joyfully imitated them all.

A song sparrow saluted the morning with a soft song. In a nest in a bush his mate was brooding five downy babies no bigger than peanuts. He kept his song low so as not to attract predators to them.

For sixteen days the male had guarded the nest while the female sat on their eggs and warmed them. She departed only to eat.

There were many other birds with babies in the woods and fields. The young mourning doves were almost as large as their parents, and under the bridge the phoebe babies were looking over the edge of their nest.

Out in the field young killdeer were flying with their parents. They had taken to their wings a few hours after hatching, for killdeer are precocious at birth. On the limb of a pine by a bridge sat four young screech owls. Their heads were still wispy with puffs of down, and their breasts were streaked with the gray of owl childhood, but they were very much on their own. At night they hunted the young mice and fat June beetles; by day, when not sleeping, they watched the fledglings of the prairie horned larks take long gliding trips over the grass tops. Hatched in late March, the little larks were flying while their parents made a nest in the alfalfa field for another brood.

As the daytime animals awoke and became busy, the butterfly crawled into the sunlight. When she could see the meadow and trees, she opened her wings and flew on.

She passed over ponds in Ohio where the young salamanders were breaking out of their egg cases and swimming among the plant stems. Gills, like ruffs, stood out from their necks, distinguishing them from frog tadpoles.

All that afternoon the monarch flew over Lake Erie and finally arrived in Canada. She came to a railroad bed where the milkweed was abundant, and here in the land where monarchs abound, she laid the last of her eggs. Toward dusk she fluttered to a pine tree by a freshwater marsh and rested.

May was not far along here. The yellow cowslips were just blooming. The arrowhead leaves were still uncurling their points to the sun, and only a few leaves of the yellow pond lilies had grown to the surface, where they would flatten on the water like paper plates. The azaleas were in bud, and the apple trees had yet to blossom.

At dusk a cheerful May chorus filled the air. Male American hop toads were singing. Their voices were tremulous and sweet as they blew their throats into tan balloons bigger than their heads. They sang for several seconds, then stopped abruptly in the manner of hop toads. The female toads listened as they sat quietly under ferns and among the new leaves of the wintergreen. Female toads do not sing; however, inspired by the chorus, one female jumped into the water. A male clasped her with his front feet, and together they drifted among the sunken sticks and leaves. The female laid a ribbon of thousands of eggs while the sperm from the male flowed over and fertilized them.

Frogs were calling, too. The tree frogs trilled, and once a bullfrog croaked. He rumbled like thunder but then stopped, for it was too early for his June courtship song.

The next day the butterfly flew on. Her wings were now small and dry. As fluids had flowed from her body into her eggs, she had shriveled. She flew slowly as she traveled beneath the tide of warblers and thrushes returning to Canada.

A wind blew her to the shores of Lake Ontario. The tatter in her wing tore deeper. Sea gulls, incubating eggs in vast colonies on the sand dunes, tilted their heads and looked up at her. Terns and

sandpipers paid her no heed as they ran in and out of the lapping water hunting small sand crabs.

The butterfly was nearly home. She had almost reached the meadow where she had been born, when suddenly a gust of wind carried her out over Lake Ontario. Her life done, she folded her wings and floated like a flower petal onto the waves.

Night came. The May moon climbed the sky. From Missouri to Canada the heirs and heiresses of the butterfly's beautiful life were beginning her story again under the moon of renewal.

Bibliography

Gibbons, Gail. *Monarch Butterfly*. New York: Holiday House, 1989.

Herberman, Ethan. *The Great Butterfly Hunt*. New York: Simon & Schuster, 1990.

Lepthien, Emilie U. *Monarch Butterflies*. Chicago: Children's Press, 1989.

Norsgaard, Jaediker E. *How to Raise Butterflies*. New York: Putnam Press, 1988.

Patent, Dorothy Winshaw. *Butterflies and Moths: How They Function*. New York: Holiday House, 1979.

Terry, Trevor. *The Life Cycle of a Butterfly*. New York: Bookwright Press, 1988.

Thompson, Susan L. *Diary of a Monarch Butterfly*. New York: Magic Circle Press, 1976.

Urquhart, Frederick A. *The Monarch Butterfly: International Traveler*. Chicago: Nelson-Hall, 1987.

Watts, Barrie. *Butterfly and Caterpillar*. Morristown, New Jersey: Silver Burdett, 1986.

Index

Arkansas, 9, 12, 29
azalea, 27, 43

bluebird, 10, 29, 31

California, 25
Canada, 12, 13, 25, 43, 44, 46
cardinal, 41
catbird, 39, 41
caterpillar, 21–22
catfish, 26, 27
chipmunk, 38
chrysalis, 22
cottontail rabbit, 36

Erie, Lake, 43

firefly, 40
fox, 36
frogs, 17, 39, 44

hop toad, 43–44

Indiana, 25, 27, 29

killdeer, 41–42

Lava Mountains, 13, 25

magnolia tree, 16–17
maple tree, 10, 13, 34
Mexico, 12, 13, 25
milkweed, 20–21, 24, 31, 33, 43

Mississippi River Valley, 9, 11, 17
Missouri, 12, 17, 46
mourning dove, 41

Ohio, 33, 42
Ohio River, 25, 27
Ontario, 12
Ontario, Lake, 44, 46

paper wasp, 31, 33
phoebe, 39, 40, 41
pine tree, 10, 14, 39, 42, 43
prairie horned lark, 42

robin, 33, 40, 41

salamander, 42
screech owl, 42
skunk, 36, 38
sparrow, 16, 41
sunfish, 17, 20

Texas, 12
thrush, 10, 31, 39, 41, 44

warbler, 10, 44
weasel, 34, 36
willow tree, 14, 33
wisteria, 12, 14, 16
wood pewee, 40